Krakow in 3 Days:

The Definitive Tourist Guide Book That Helps You Travel Smart and Save Time

"Finest City Guides"

Book Description

Krakow in some ways seems like a city from an old fairy tale. When you walk the cobbled streets, you will see a bell tower and magnificent churches, and a stalwart castle outside town. The experience of Europe is alive here. **Krakow in 3 Days** is of great help to you, since you may only have several days to spend here.

Inside, we'll share with you:

- How to get to Krakow by air
- What currency you'll need
- How to pay and when to tip
- Accommodations for every budget
- Neighborhoods you may want to visit
- How to get around while you're in town
- The best attractions
- Places you'll want to eat

So, let us guide you through this town that speaks of Old Europe.

The People of Krakow

The people who live in this "city from the past" are usually friendly and helpful. Poles now relish differences in ethnicities, where once they would not welcome someone who was not "like them", in appearance or otherwise.

Poland was closed off from the world for many years, with the communists keeping it sheltered but shuttered. After communism fell, her gates were flung open, and the world finally started to discover the cities of Poland, like Krakow and Warsaw.

Krakow does have tourists, but it isn't as crowded as some European cities. You can walk down the streets without getting caught in crowds. The Old Town of Krakow has many locals who shop there as well as tourists, and many travelers enjoy integrating with locals, rather than always being in crowds with other tourists.

Language

The native language of the country and the city is Polish. English is spoken by many younger people, however. German is also common. Other languages you may hear include Kashubian, Belarusian, Rusyn, Lithuanian, Slovak and Czech. More widely dispersed, some people speak Ukrainian, Romani, Armenian or Hungarian.

Holidays

Jan 1	New Year's Day	National holiday
January	Epiphany	National holiday
Feb 14	Valentine's Day	Observance
March	March equinox	Season
April	Good Friday	Observance
April	Holy Saturday	Observance
April	Easter Day	National holiday
April	Easter Monday	National holiday

May 1	Labor Day / May Day	National holiday
May 3	Constitution Day	National holiday
May	Mother's Day	Observance
June	Whit Sunday	National holiday
June	Corpus Christi	National holiday
June	June Solstice	Season
June	Father's Day	Observance
August	Assumption of Mary	National holiday
September	September equinox	Season
Nov 1	All Saints' Day	National holiday
Nov 11	Independence Day	National holiday
December	December Solstice	Season
Dec 24	Christmas Eve	Observance
Dec 25	Christmas Day	National holiday
Dec 26	Second Day of Christmas	National holiday
Dec 31	New Year's Eve	Observance

Religious Beliefs

When you speak of religion in Poland, many people think of Catholicism. Roughly 90% of the people who claim a religion in Poland are Roman Catholics. That percentage is certainly not exact, since it counts all baptized Catholics, some of which worship in different religions now. Catholicism is still the religion most widely taught in Polish schools.

Other religions practiced in Poland are still mostly Christian, and they include Orthodox Christians, Byzantine Catholics, Evangelicals, Old Believers, Seventh-Day Adventists, Methodists, Jehovah's Witnesses and Pentecostals.

There are smaller communities of Jews, Muslims, Hare Krishna's and Karaims. As you can see, there are many non-Catholic religions practiced, but the numbers who practice these other religions are fairly small.

Here is a quick preview of what you will learn in this tourist guide:

- Helpful information about Krakow
- Flying into the city
- Transportation tips in town
- Why Krakow is such a vibrant tourist spot and what you will find most remarkable about it
- Information on luxury and budget accommodations
- The currency used in Krakow
- Tourist attractions you should make time to see
- Other attractions for entertainment and culture
- Events that may be running during your stay
- Tips on the best places to eat & drink for all price points, whether you want simple fare, worldwide dishes or Polish flavor

Table of Contents

Introduction

Krakow is the second largest (by population) city in Poland, and the main destination of tourists in the country. Production and industry still provide much of their jobs, but they are seeing a growth in service industries like shopping, hotels, restaurants, etc.

The city of Krakow is considered to be Poland's cultural capital, with seven universities and almost 20 other higher learning institutions in the city. The academic nature makes Krakow the main center of education and science in Poland.

There is so much fine architecture in Krakow that you could almost spend your entire trip visiting churches and other buildings of the same era. However, we have given you a broad base of attractions, so that you can experience more fully all the things Krakow has to offer.

A Brief History of Krakow

Archaeologically speaking, evidence has shown that even back to the Paleolithic period, humans had settled in the area that is now called Krakow. Archeologists have found stone tools near Wawel Hill that date to 50,000 BC.

Poland's mysterious earthen mounds were most likely constructed in the 600s AD. Historians have dated the Old Town of Krakow as slightly newer, probably being built in the 700s.

Late in the 9th century, Moravians ruled the area around what is now Krakow, before it was held under Bohemian rule. After this time, Krakow was incorporated into the Piast dynasty, and the Kingdom of Poland was created. By 966 AD, Krakow was already a busy center of commerce.

The city would develop rapidly during this time, and became the country's capital city in 1038. Krakow was invaded three times by Mongols in the 13th century, and rebuilt each time. After the last invasion, the people built three kilometers (nearly two miles) of defensive gates, walls and towers. They were modernized during the next several centuries.

The prosperity of Krakow continued during the Polish-Lithuanian rule of the Jagiello dynasty, from 1386 to 1572. Talented scientists, artists and humanists came from Germany and Italy, creating impressive buildings, frescos, sculptures and other works of art.

When King Zygmunt II died in 1572, he did not leave an heir, and the importance of Krakow to the region declined. Warsaw became the capital of Poland in 1596. The Swedish invasion during the 1600s resulted in the pillaging of Krakow, and the city lost 20,000 residents to the plague known as the black death in Europe.

Late in the 1700s, after the United States had passed its democratic constitution (the first in the world), Poland passed theirs. The country was still invaded by Austria, Russia and Prussia in the days following the signing of the constitution, and for years afterwards.

Krakow became the bastion of the rebels who fought foreign invaders. Later in the 1700s, Tadeusz Kościuszko, a Polish freedom-fighter, started an insurrection in the Market Square, although it ultimately failed. The Prussians looted the royal treasury. Krakow became a part of Austria at that time.

While under Austria's rule, the city walls of Krakow were levelled, except for several sections. The Austrians were more lenient rulers than Prussia or Russia, and Krakow again became a center of nationalism on Poland. Modernization also occurred during this time, and the city saw its first electric streetcars, electricity in homes and running water.

When WW I broke out, the city was set upon by Russian troops, and many people fled Krakow. The city was liberated from Austrian rule in 1918, after a planned revolt. The first sovereign state of Poland was established in the Treaty of Versailles.

The peace would not last. In 1939, forces from Nazi Germany invaded Krakow and set up their general government there, at Wawel Castle. During WW II, more than 150 professors from the Jagiellonian University were sent to concentration camps.

The Jewish people in the Kazimierz ghetto of Krakow were sent to concentration and work camps nearby. The people who lived in the Jewish ghetto in the city were eradicated in town, sent to death in Auschwitz or sent to work camps.

The liberation of Krakow from the Germans came in 1945, with the architecture of the city still nearly intact. After WW II, the Polish experienced nearly 45 years of communism.

In 1989, the Solidarity trade union of Krakow forced free elections. Lech Walesa, a freedom fighter, was elected the first president of Poland, post-Communism. Since the city was much more well-preserved than others in Europe during WW II, it stands as one of the most important cultural and historical artifacts of Poland. The city saw 12 million tourists in 2016.

Neighborhoods

Podgórze

This area was once an outpost for the Austrians, competing with Krakow, before being incorporated eventually into the city itself. After the opening of the footbridge in 2010, this district came back to life, and even though its past saw much turmoil, it is a unique and interesting part of the city, steeped in history.

Kazimierz

This area is sometimes called the "SoHo" of Krakow. It boasts nightclubs and fine museums, boutiques and eateries. It has its own unique culture and history. Each evening and weekend night, trendy residents party on Plac Nowy and other side streets. In some ways, it is still in many ways its own city within the larger city.

Zablocie

This is an industrial area in the throes of a boom, much like Berlin or New York City once had. New clubs, cafes, museums and even apartments have sprung up in old alleyways, lofts and factories.

Stare Miasto

This is the beating heart of Krakow, where you can mix with locals. It's the largest of all medieval town squares in all of Europe. You'll find many bars, cafes and eateries here. You'll always find something to do (or eat).

What does Krakow offer its Visitors?

Krakow may surprise you with the breadth of things there are to see and do. Everyone knows about the concentration camps, but sadness isn't the only feeling you'll experience in this town. In addition to having friendly residents and cheap food, drink and hotels, it's a unique city.

Krakow's cobbled streets and elegant buildings won't disappoint those who are history buffs or architecture aficionados. You can do a lot of exploring of the Old Town on foot, and public transportation is inexpensive, too.

Krakow has many attractions you won't want to miss, including monuments, magnificent churches, and many relics, historic as well as contemporary.

1. Key Information about Krakow

Money Matters

Poland is in the European Union, but it also has its own currency. Zloty is its legal tender. Some places also accept euros as payment. Zloty is abbreviated to zl and PLN.

One zloty is divided into 100 smaller units known as grosz.

Polish money comes in these denominations:

Coins: 1, 2,5, 10, 20 and 50 grosz, and 1, 2 and 5 zloty coins.

Bank Notes: 10, 20, 50, 100, 200 and 500 zloty.

Most moneychangers (kantors) in Poland are honest and offer good rates. Check the current exchange rate online on your phone and compare with the rate you are offered. It's best not to exchange currency at the airport. ATMs are useful for pulling out the proper currency.

Tipping

Whether you tip or not in Poland depends on what type of service you receive. You are not obliged to tip, but it is customarily done to show that you appreciate good service.

Most people tip in hotels, as long as the service was good. You should not feel like you have to, though. Many Polish hotels don't have bellboys and porters. Hotel housekeepers do not expect you to tip, but they'll certainly appreciate 10PLN left on the bedside table or bed. If your concierge provides any extra services like booking a tour or something like that, you can give him 20 PLN in an envelope as you leave. It's not expected, but it is appreciated.

Restaurant Tipping

A tip is expected if you have good service and food in a Polish restaurant, particularly in areas that cater to tourists, like many places in

Krakow. The usual tip is 10% of your bill. If you had exceptional service, you could tip 15%.

You may hand your tip to the waiter or leave it on your table. If you pay for your bill using a credit card, leave a cash tip if you can, or it will be kept by the owner. If you have bad service, do not tip.

2. Transport to and in Krakow

Getting to Krakow by Plane

You will fly into John Paul II International Airport when you go to Krakow. The airport is actually found in Balice Village, about seven miles from downtown Krakow. It's the second busiest airport in Poland.

Getting to Krakow from the Airport

Buses

Public transport buses link the airport to the city. They arrive every 30 minutes during the day, and less often at night. It is the cheapest way to get into the city. The cost from the airport to the city center is 4 PLN ($1.10 USD) without any transfers, to 5 PLN ($1.37 USD), which allows for tram or bus transfers within an hour after boarding.

You can use public buses after you buy tickets from a machine in the airport arrival hall, or at the bus stop (you can use credit card or cash). Most buses have ticket machines on board, but these usually will take coins only. Be sure to validate your ticket as soon as you board a bus.

You can also find privately-owned minibuses and buses that connect the airport to the center of Krakow, and to other cities. These may require advance bookings.

Trains

The suburban line SKA1 runs from the airport to the main rail station. It takes less than 20 minutes, generally, to get from the airport to the center of town. The price from airport to the city center is 9 PLN ($2.46 USD).

You can purchase tickets from machines on each platform, in arrivals hall and sometimes on the train or from onboard staff (cash only).

Krakow Rental Cars

There are various locations where you can rent a car for your trip. They have names you know like Budget, Avis, Ace, Alamo, AutoEurope, Dollar and Enterprise. Most of the attractions are in or near the Old Town, and taxis are inexpensive, so you likely won't need to pay for a rental car.

The only trip that most tourists take out of town is to the concentration and work camps, mainly Auschwitz. These are sold by tour companies, and they have their own buses. You really can't get the same experience by driving there and wandering the sad camps yourself. There is special parking for tour groups and confusing signage that may make it more difficult, if you go on your own.

Krakow Cabs

Krakow Airport Taxi is the single official taxi company at the airport. You can book them online. They accept credit cards. Charges within various zones for taxis are the same, regardless of how long the ride takes. Day of the week and time of day also do not affect the flat fare.

Taxis in town

Taxis should always have a sign on the roof that says "Taxi". There are also stickers in the rear windows. The initial charge is between PLN 5-7 (USD $1.37- $1.91), and then there is a charge per km of PLN 2-3 (USD 55 cents to 82 cents)

Local car services like MaxiDriver, iCar or Car-o usually cost less than the taxis do, and they will quote you a price in advance, based on the actual distance from your location to your desired destination. 8km rides cost about PLN 22 ($6 USD).

Payment and Tipping for Taxi's

You'll pay your taxi fare when you reach your destination. Most taxis are equipped to accept credit cards. It's a good idea to carry cash, just in case.

Tipping etiquette for taxis in Poland is to leave a 10% tip if your taxi arrives on time and takes the proper, not roundabout route. If your taxi is late, or slow, it's not normal to tip at all.

Public Transport in Krakow

Krakow has an extensive public transportation system that uses bus and tram lines. Rush hours for daily commuters are generally between 7-9 AM and 5-7 PM.

You may purchase otickets before you board, using a ticket machine, kiosk or bus/tram stop. These are found mainly in the center of town and offer help in several languages.

Some buses and trams have ticket machines onboard. They are marked with the letter "A" above their entrance. A PLN5 ticket can be bought from the drivers, but you will need to pay exact change.

Be sure to have your ticket validated. Fines can be as high as PLN150 if tickets are not validated.

Passes & Tickets

A one-way tram or bus ticket is PLN 3.8 (USD $1.04). They can be purchased at ticket machines, downtown stops and newsstands. Tram and bus drivers sell 1-hour tickets that are worth PLN 5 ($1.37 USD). After you board and validate your ticket, keep your ticket with you.

Unlimited travel passes for trams and buses are available by day. The three-day pass is PLN36 ($9.85 USD). These passes are valid for the stated time period, starting with the first time they are punched on a tram or bus. You won't punch the pass again until you're done with it. These passes are good in the city only.

3. Accommodations

Krakow is adding and refurbishing many hotels and other accommodations for the tourists who are discovering the city. There are very few exclusive hotels, and a great many inexpensive ones. The prices are extremely reasonable, especially compared to many other cities in Europe.

Prices for luxury hotels: $190 USD per night and up

Kanonicza 22

- In Old Town, close to St. Mary's basilica, Wawel Cathedral, Main Market Square and Wawel Castle

Hotel Elektor

- Close to the Main Market Square, Florianska Street, St. Mary's Basilica Czartoryski Museum and Florian's Gate

Hotel Stary

- In Old Town, close to Cloth Hall, Main Market Square, St. Mary's Basilica and Town Hall Tower

Palace Apartments – Prestige

- Close to Wawel Castle, Main Market Square, Czartoryski Museum Florian's Gate and Krakow Barbican

Old Town Luxury Apartments by Amstra

- Close to Wawel Castle, Main Market Square, Czartoryski Museum, Florian's Gate and Krakow Barbican

Wawel Apartments Sarego Residence

- Close to Main Market Square, St. Mary's Basilica, Galicia Jewish Museum, Old Synagogue and Wawel Castle

Prices for Mid-Range Hotels - $120 USD to $175 USD per night

Hotel Copernicus

- In Old Town, close to Cloth Hall, Wawel Castle, St. Mary's Basilica, Wawel Cathedral and Main Market Square

Grand Ascot Hotel

- Close to St. Mary' Basilica, Cloth Hall, Town Hall Tower, Collegium Maius and Main Market Square

Bonerowski Palace

- In Old Town, close to Czartoryski Museum, Town Hall Tower, Cloth Hall, St. Mary's Basilica and Main Market Square

Orlowska Townhouse

- In Old Town, close to Town Hall Tower, Krakow Barbican, Florian's Gate, Czartoryski Museum and Main Market Square

Sheraton Grand Krakow

- In the Heart of Krakow, close to Town Hall Tower, Cloth Hall, Wawel Cathedral, Main Market Square and Wawel Castle

Prices for Budget Hotels: Less than $100 USD per night

Hilton Garden Inn Krakow Airport

- Close to Park Decjusza, Main Market Square, Pilsudski's Mound, Wolski Forest and Collegium Maius

Q Hotel Krakow, BW Premier Collection

- Close to Galicia Jewish Museum, Old Synagogue, Wawel Cathedral, Main Market Square and Wawel Castle

Apartmenty InPoint

- In Heart of Krakow, close to St. Mary's Basilica, Wawel Castle, Main Market Square, Galicia Jewish Museum and Old Synagogue

Hotel B.A.S. Villa Residence

- Close to Czartoryski Museum, Florian's Gate, Krakow Barbican, Wawel Castle and Main Market Square

Cracowdays

- In the Heart of Krakow, close to Cloth Hall, Main Market Square, Town Hall Tower and Wawel Castle

Petrus Hotel

- Close to Wawel Cathedral, Town Hall Tower, Wawel Castle, Cloth Hall and Main Market Square

4. Sightseeing

From historic attractions to shopping, dining and nightclubbing, Krakow has you covered. Many people choose to take tour the Auschwitz-Birkenau Memorial & Museum, although it may not a particularly good choice if you have young children along.

Enthusiasts of old architecture will enjoy St. Mary's Basilica and the Wawel Cathedral. You can spend much of your time in Old Town and the Main Market Square. When you're tired from walking, relax and get something to eat or drink and people-watch – always an interesting pastime in almost any country.

Auschwitz Birkenau Guided Tour - Memorial and Museum

The Auschwitz Birkenau Tour allows you to visit and learn more about arguably the best known of the Nazi concentration camps. The Germans killed 1.5 million people in acts of genocide in WW II.

Tours include a bus ride to the camps, a visit to Auschwitz I, which was the administration center of the death camp, and a tour of Auschwitz II, which was designed and built as a facility for extermination. It is a living testament to the evil that men can act out on others. For most Krakow visitors, this is considered a "must-see".

The guided tour includes:

- Hotel pick up & drop off
- 7-hour total trip time from Krakow
- English-speaking tour leaders
- A documentary during the bus ride

Main Square

The Main Square of Krakow is nearly always bustling with locals and tourists. It's truly the heart of the city – you can feel the pulse. Many political events and festivals are held there. When you want to escape some of the activity, check out St. Mary's Basilica, which is located just off the square.

Krakow Cloth Hall – Shopping

This has been called the oldest shopping mall in the world. It's been open for about 700 years, in Grand Square. In the 1300s, a roof was built over the two stall rows, forming Cloth Hall, which was the center for textile trading. Today, many stall owners sell different types of souvenirs. Don't leave Cloth Hall without heading upstairs to the museum.

Krakow National Museum

Upstairs from the Cloth Hall, this museum exhibits an unrivaled collection of Polish art from the 19th century. There is also a café on this level, and it is a wonderful place with a roof terrace that overlooks the central square of Old Town.

Town Hall Tower Krakow

It is believed that the Town Hall Tower was built in the early 1300s. It was expanded on in the Middle Ages. The tower was a part of the Cracow City Hall that was demolished in the beginning of the 1400s.

The tower was repaired, and equipped in 1524 with a Nuremburg-produced clock. When lightning struck the tower in the late 1600s, it caused a fire that burned half the tower, and the bell. It was reconstructed within three years.

5. Eat & Drink

Poland's rich farmland is the source of cereal grains that form one of the staples of the Polish diet. They include barley, buckwheat, wheat and rye. They are used in dumplings, noodles, dark bread and other frequently eaten foods in Poland.

Other agricultural products of importance include cucumbers, mushrooms, carrots, cabbage, beets and potatoes. The main side dish is often boiled potatoes, eaten with fish, meat or poultry. Cucumber salads are another Polish staple.

The chefs of Poland utilize the ingredients above and many more, which are locally sourced when possible. You can eat to your heart's delight in Krakow. The prices can't be beat, even for fine dining.

Fine Dining Restaurants

Wierzynek – approximately $68 USD for two

This is a relatively new restaurant, comparatively speaking. The service is excellent, and it is said that the servers can read the customers' minds on what they would like to eat. Suffice to say that they know which dishes will please people the most.

Among the most popular dishes here are ox, geese, duck and deer. The Roe Deer and Quail Duet must be eaten if you expect to taste perhaps the most tender meat you've ever eaten.

Restauracja Amarylis – approximately $60 USD for two

The décor in this popular restaurant is a wonderful accompaniment to the dishes they serve. The wait staff is attentive without hovering over you.

The favorite soups include chicken and beetroot. They're quite tasty and flavorful. As far as mains are concerned, it's hard to top the duck breast and veal with campfire potatoes. The desserts are well-known, too, including crème brulee and original chocolate chip cookies.

Cyrano de Bergerac – approximately $41 USD for two

Located in the cellar of its building, there is an excellent atmosphere for dining here. They do well in pairing wines with meals. The favorite dishes include quail consommé, pigeon and beef wellington. The meat is tender, and cooked to perfection.

Pod Nosem – approximately $46 USD for two

This is a wonderful place if you're a culinary aficionado who wishes to taste original and unique variations on the local cuisine. They offer excellent service in a historic interior. You might like to try their wild boar, liver, broad beans and quail eggs.

Mid-Range Restaurants

Piastowska – approximately $39 USD for two

This is an exquisite dining experience for visitors and locals alike. They offer appetizers that include ham wrapped in a horse radish cream sauce, and mains including Silesian dumplings, pork ham and braised tenderloin. Try their desserts – they make a great apple pie, served with whipped cream and ice cream.

Trzej Kucharze – approximately $34 USD for two

The wait staff at this popular restaurant are always close by, and attentive to your needs. The food is well-seasoned and fresh, and there are generous portions.

Among the favorite dishes are salmon, pancakes with fruit and turkey papilotach. The meats are delicate and fragile. For dessert, many people enjoy the chocolate nut cake, with excellent decoration and quite a tasty experience.

Zielone Tarasy – approximately $27 USD for two

From repeat customers, you'll learn that this inviting restaurant has comfortable surroundings and first-class service. The favorite soups include pumpkin, mushroom cream, lentil or tomato cream. Other recommended dishes include minced cutlets with salad, fried onion and potatoes and pork loin or rolled pork tenderloin with potatoes or rice.

Dynia Resto Bar – approximately $22 USD for two

You'll be amazed at the sheer size of this restaurant, but they usually seat guests in the back first, and that area is well-lit, yet personal. Try the spicy eggplant rolls with basil pesto and feta in tomato sauce. The Resto Bar is also known for its salads, including fresh spinach lettuce with chicken and melon and their marinated chicken salad with raspberry vinaigrette, vegetables, pears and gorgonzola.

Cheap Eats

Stylowa – approximately $16 USD for two

In Nowa Huta district, just east of Old Town, this is an authentic Polish restaurant. It's a local legend since the Polish communist years, and it's a must-visit place if you're interested in the culinary and political history of Poland. Among their favorite traditional Polish dishes is veal escallops with buckwheat in mushroom sauce.

Karczma Pod Blachą – approximately $11 USD for two

The garden here is the most popular place to eat, and the waitresses dress in folk costumes, to add to the authenticity. They make wonderful, authentic Polish meals like mixed platters, various meats, mountain cheese with red berry and pierogis. You'll get the feel for their genuine Polish food.

Pod Srebrnym Kurem – approximately $8 USD for two

This pub has great food, along with beer and drinks. Their servers will be happy to recommend menu items for you. Check out their chicken broth, and borscht and camembert cheese. The cheese is tastiest, according to regular diners, and the pork chops are very good, too.

Tavolino – approximately $9 USD for two

The décor in this Italian bistro is neat and simple and the wait staff is friendly – they always have a smile for you. The pizzas are plenty large enough for two people, with extra left over. They have thick crust pizza with lots of sauces. Locals recommend Pepperoni, Tropical and Europa pizzas.

6. Culture and Entertainment

Krakow is home to many historical monuments and buildings of art and culture. It is an attractive tourist destination and you can do more for less money than you can in many other European cities.

Krakow offers you theaters, museums, galleries and festivals that will help you to learn more about the culture of this region in Poland.

Wawel Hill and Castle

People in Krakow are justifiably proud of this ancient seat for kings of Poland. The castle is an excellent example of a building of Baroque architecture. Wawel Hill transitioned from a stronghold of pagans to the seat of a powerful medieval nation.

Saint Mary's Basilica

You'll find St. Mary's on the east side of Krakow's Main Market Square. It was built in a Gothic style in the 1200s. Tatars destroyed the basilica, but it was rebuilt during the 1300s. Its two towers are of different heights and styles, making them quite unique in historical architecture.

The highlight of St. Mary's Basilica is the wooden alter piece near the entrance for visitors. The panels on this alter depict scenes from the bible, including Jesus' Ascension.

"Wieliczka" Salt Mine

What started out as a working salt mine ran for centuries, but closed as a mining operation in 2007. Since then, however, it has become a major attraction for people who visit Krakow, and a UNESCO World Heritage site. The highlight of the mine is a temple, made entirely of salt, underground.

While extensively popular, this tour is quite a walk. There are 800 steps in the mine that lead to the carved sculptures and temple, some going down and some going back up to the elevator after the tour.

Rynek Underground Permanent Exhibition

Under the market square of Krakow is the 7100+ square yard central museum. At a cost of 38 million zloty (over $8 million USD), it was started in 2009. When it opened in 2010, it only displayed regular exhibitions.

The main exhibit shows the European identity of Krakow, and uses holograms and fog machines to make you feel as though you have traveled back 700 years to an earlier city. There are touchscreens in the museum that allow you to see 600 models in 3D.

Botanical Garden of the Jagiellonian University

Jagiellonian University's Botanic Garden was founded in the late 1700s. It can be found just east of Old Town. It includes three greenhouses, where many plants are displayed, and you can visit two of them. You may enjoy the tropical plant display, which includes plants that produce ginger, cocoa, tea and coffee.

Krakow Night-Life

If you have any interest in late night revelry, you may want to experience the nightlife of Krakow. It's known as the most partying city in Poland for a reason, after all. There are many clubs, bars and pubs that stay open until nearly daylight, and they offer drinks mainly on the inexpensive side. There are many types of music played, along with yummy street food and unique events to enjoy.

Kazimierz (Jewish Quarter)

This area may seem cozy during the daylight hours, and it is charming but bustling at night. It is often described as Bohemian or hipster-like, and includes restaurants, bars and cafes with places to party and enjoy music. Kazimierz offers all-night dance sessions and alternative bands, along with cheap food and drinks.

Main Market Square

This is a very popular area at night – nearly as popular as it is in the daytime hours. Almost all the historical buildings have restaurants, pubs or clubs, and there are clubs underground, as well. Most of the Main Market Square clubs are open until 5 AM, with wide selections of drinks, and good discounts.

Plaza Krakow

This is such a unique place to party the night away! It's like heading to the beach, but you never have to leave the city. You can lounge in beach chairs in warm sand, overlooking Wawel Hill and Kazimierz while you sip a cocktail or a beer. They also offer main dishes and finger foods. You can even enjoy swimming in a pool, located in a river barge.

7. Special Events in Krakow

International Shanty Festival
February

This is the largest sea song festival found anywhere in Europe. Top stars that specialize in this type of music are featured.

Misteria Paschalia Festival
March/April

This event has been held annually since 2004. It is among Europe's most outstanding events focused on Baroque and Renaissance music. The ideal music at this festival is the presentation of masterpieces linked somehow to Holy Week or Easter.

The Krakow Film Festival   May/June

The film festival in Krakow was first organized in 1961. It is devoted to short films, animation films and documentaries.

Summer Jazz Festival   **July**

First held in 1996, the Piwnica Pod Baranami Cabaret holds many of the performances for the jazz festival. There are also events at the Radio Krakow Auditorium, Krakow's Opera House and the Krakow Philharmonic. Additional music celebrations are held at art galleries and theaters, as well as in an open-air setting at the Main Market and on the grounds of the Archeological Museum. There are roughly 60 concerts in total, with artists from Poland and other countries.

The Night of Museums   **May**

On this night, the museums in Krakow remain open long past the evening time, with additional attractions for locals and visitors alike. The tickets are usually only 1PLN (about 28 cents US).

Music in Old Krakow   August

This is one of Poland's oldest festivals. Traditional culture in Krakow has created an aura that is conducive to performing music. In addition to showcasing famous musical artists, the festival also provides an opportunity for young, new and talented musicians to perform. The concerts themselves are held at various venues, most of them historical.

Sacrum Profanum Festival
September/October

This contemporary music festival was introduced to break down barriers and change people's perception of modern and contemporary music. It's billed as a musical journey that will take you through indie classic and avant-garde music.

Zaduszki Jazz Festival   November

This is the oldest jazz festival in Europe. It features jazz musicians from Poland and the international stage, as well.

Christmas Market   **December**

There is a special, indefinable atmosphere in Krakow's Main Market Square in the days leading up to Christmas. You can peruse great food, Christmas ornaments, toys, knitted wear, candies, pottery and souvenirs.

New Year's Eve in Main Market Square December/January

December 31 brings thousands of locals and visitors to Market Square. (Bundle up – it's cold!) There, the evening starts with free rock concerts. Just before the clock strikes midnight, they begin a countdown, and as St. Mary's Cathedral bells ring 12 AM, the fireworks are set off into the winter sky.

8. Safety in Krakow

Poland is safer, as a rule, than most countries in Europe, and Krakow is among Poland's safest cities. Normal precautions and common sense will likely keep you perfectly safe.

Petty crime is rather common in the city, however. We're not talking muggings, but pilferage and pickpocketing. Car theft is a problem, although it is declining, and isn't an issue for most tourists, since they use public transit and taxis to get around.

There are two types of police people who patrol Krakow. The state police, or Policja, is the national law enforcement body. You may also see municipal guards, which are Krakow police. The local police do not have as much authority as the Policja.

Safety Tips
Be keenly aware of potential pickpockets in all crowded places, especially on public transit and

when in shops, or at bus stops, railroad stations and the airport.

As with any large tourist town, keep your passport, money and credit cards in the safe in your room or a money belt, when you need them. If you carry any type of handbag, keep a tight grip on it and hold it close to your body.

If you travel by train, avoid raucous passengers and empty compartments.

Keep an eye on your luggage at the airport, bus depots, railroad stations and on the train or bus.

Don't allow strangers to give you drinks from their water bottle or other beverage carrier, especially not alcoholic beverages.

If you're at a nightclub, keep your hand on your drink. Don't make new friends right on the streets, and keep on well-lit streets at night.

Don't buy anything on the street, especially not something that is supposed to be valuable.

Conclusion

Krakow may not be the first city that you ponder when you're thinking about a vacation. But give it a chance. It's so much more than just a city. You need to spend time there (even if it's only a few days) to appreciate its charm and uniqueness.

As soon as you walk in the Main Market Square, you'll become relaxed and optimistic, since many of your hours will be spent in this enchanting area. There are lively bars, restaurants, cafes and shops along the outside of the square and on nearby streets.

We have given you:
- A selection of hotels in various price ranges
- The attractions you will want to make time for
- Restaurant options, sorted by price range, so you can try different cuisines
- Helpful tips to stay safe and enjoy your trip
- How to make the most of your three days in Krakow

Printed in Great Britain
by Amazon

50171364R00033